ANIMAL ALPHABET

BERT KITCHEN

A PUFFIN PIED PIPER

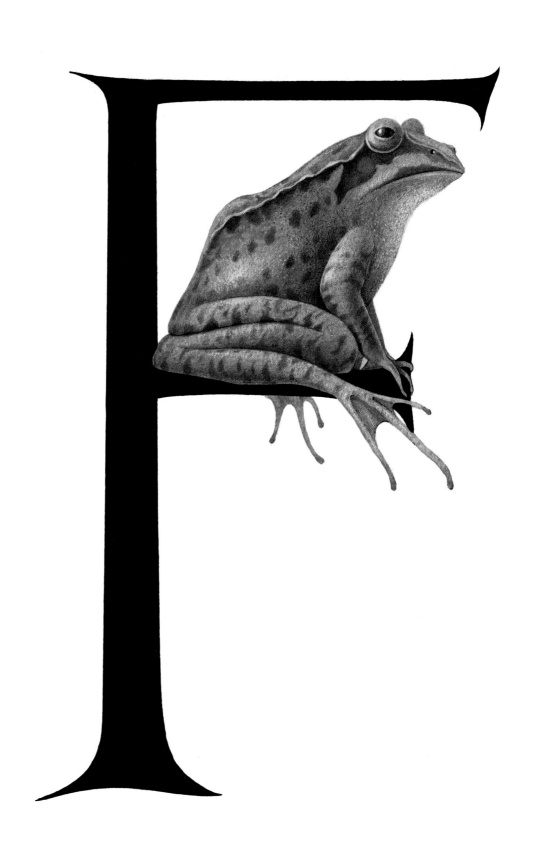

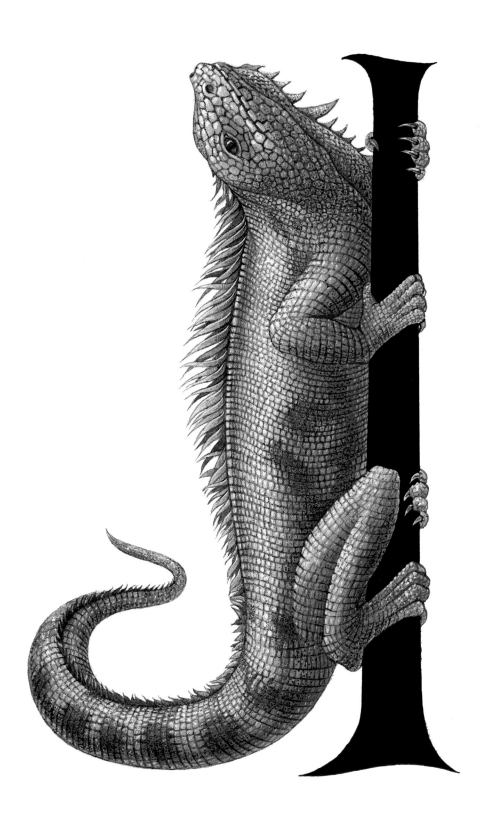

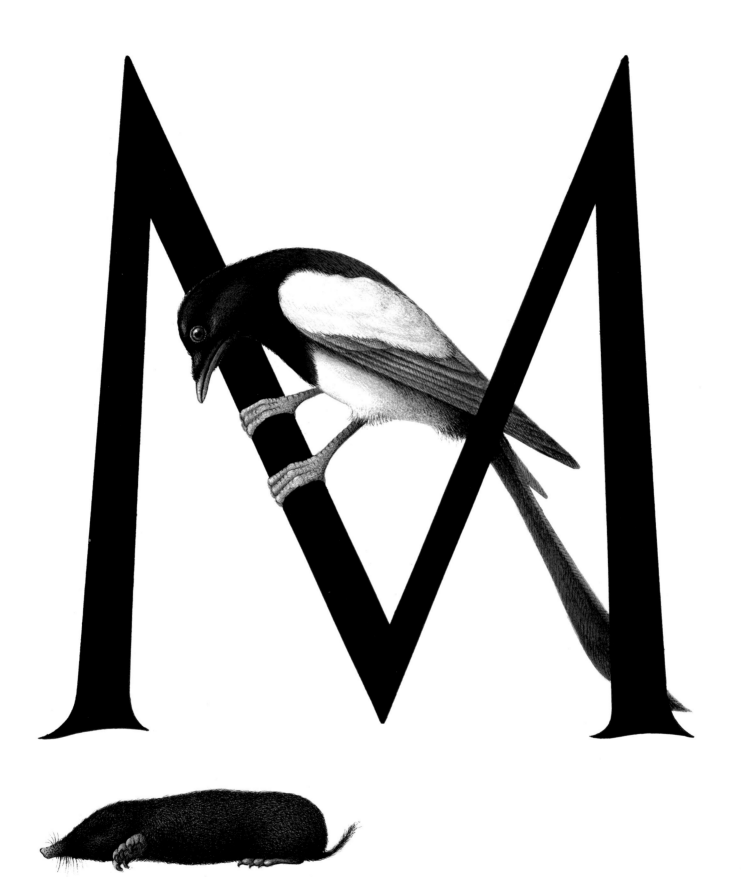

ANIMAL ANSWERS

A	Armadillo (Nine-banded)	**N**	Newt
B	Bat	**O**	Ostrich
C	Chameleon (Mediterranean)	**P**	Penguin (Rockhopper)
D	Dodo	**Q**	Quetzal
E	Elephant	**R**	Rhinoceros
F	Frog	**S**	Snail
G	Giraffe	**T**	Tortoise
H	Hedgehog	**U**	Umbrella Bird
I	Iguana	**V**	Vulture (Ruppell's)
J	Jerboa	**W**	Walrus
K	Koala	**X**	X-ray Fish (Pristella riddlei)
L	Lion	**Y**	Yak
M	Magpie (Pica pica) and Mole	**Z**	Zebra (chapman's)

for Corinna and Saskia

First published in the United States 1984 by Dial Books
A Division of Penguin Books USA Inc.
375 Hudson Street
New York, New York 10014

Published in Great Britain by Lutterworth Press
Copyright © 1984 by Bert Kitchen
All rights reserved
Library of Congress Catalog Card Number: 83-23929
Printed in Hong Kong by South China Printing Co.
First Pied Piper Printing 1988
(c)
5 7 9 10 8 6 4

A Pied Piper Book is a registered trademark of
Dial Books, a division of Penguin Books USA Inc.,
® TM 1,163,686 and ® TM 1,054,312.

ANIMAL ALPHABET
is published in a hardcover edition by
Dial Books.
ISBN 0-14-054601-4